JUDE BELLINGHAM

BEN LERWILL

FOOTBALL LEGENDS

JUDE BELLINGHAM

SCHOLASTIC

Published in the UK by Scholastic, 2024
1 London Bridge, London, SE1 9BG
Scholastic Ireland, 89E Lagan Road, Dublin Industrial Estate, Glasnevin,
Dublin, D11 HP5F

Text © Ben Lerwill, 2024
Cover illustration © Stanley Chow, 2024

ISBN 978 0702 33742 0

A CIP catalogue record for this book is available from the British Library.

Printed and bound in Great Britain by Clays Ltd, Elcograf S.p.A

Paper made from wood grown in sustainable
forests and other controlled sources.

MIX
Paper | Supporting
responsible forestry
FSC® C018072
FSC
www.fsc.org

1 3 5 7 9 10 8 6 4 2

www.scholastic.co.uk

Contents

30 OCTOBER, 2023

It was a dark and drizzly night in Paris. Taxis swished down the avenues. People hurried home along the pavements.

But in a grand theatre in the heart of the French city, something special was taking place. The theatre was packed with people in smart suits and elegant dresses – people who usually wore sweaty shirts and muddy boots. The 2023 *Ballon d'Or* ceremony had started, and the biggest footballers on the planet were gathered together. The air was buzzing with excitement.

Kylian Mbappé and Lionel Messi were there.

Aitana Bonmatí and Mary Earps, too. Kevin de Bruyne, Erling Haaland and Vinícius Júnior were sitting near icons like David Beckham, Didier Drogba and Gary Lineker. There were big names everywhere, row after row of the world's best footballers and managers, all in one place, all looking at the same stage.

In the middle of it all, a twenty-year-old from the West Midlands sat in his front row seat and tried to stay calm.

The moment had come to hear who had won the *Kopa* Trophy, the award for the world's best young player over the previous twelve months. The trophy was extra special because it had been voted for by former *Ballon d'Or* winners. Superstars such as Lionel Messi, Cristiano Ronaldo, Karim Benzema and Zinedine Zidane had chosen who would win.

Tonight, there were some incredible young footballers on the shortlist, all waiting anxiously to hear the result. They included world-class players like Jamal Musiala, Pedri and Eduardo Camavinga – plus, of course, the youngster from the West Midlands.

A familiar figure walked onstage to present the trophy. It was Eden Hazard, a winger who had won Europe's biggest club trophies during his career. He was a fitting choice for handing over such a prestigious award.

Eden was holding an envelope containing the winner's name. And as the theatre held its breath, he opened it and started to read. "So, the *Kopa* Trophy goes to…" He paused, looked down at the envelope, then smiled, "Jude Bellingham."

The twenty-year-old in the front row felt a rush of joy. Music started playing as the audience broke into loud applause. Jude rose from his seat and walked to the stage, savouring the moment.

Seconds later he was up there in the spotlight, with the eyes of the theatre staring up at him. He might have been young, but he stood almost a full head taller than Eden Hazard. As the applause continued, he was handed the trophy and went across to the microphone.

Wow, he thought, as he looked out at the sea of faces. *Is this all real?* Only a few years ago he'd been playing as a substitute in the Championship. Now he'd just been voted the best young player on

Planet Earth.

"Good evening everyone," he said, feeling slightly nervous, but soon sounding more confident. "I just want to thank everyone who's helped me get to this point: Birmingham City, Borussia Dortmund, Real Madrid and the England national team. And, most importantly, my family – my mum, my dad and my brother."

He took a breath and continued. "Thank you for all the support, it means a lot," he said, then he gave a small smile. "And there's more to come."

The rest of the evening was a blur. The congratulations came thick and fast. There were pats on the back, handshakes, hugs, selfies with fans, camera flashes and interviews. By the time he got back to his hotel room with his trophy Jude was elated but exhausted.

Now he could relax. He looked in the bathroom mirror and let his mind settle. He had just won the *Kopa* Trophy. No way! What a journey his career had been. He was still only twenty, but already the whole of the football world knew his name.

Life moves fast. He knew that better than anyone.

He stared at the trophy again, then gave a happy sigh as he thought about the current season. In just a few days' time he would be back on the pitch for Real Madrid, playing in the Santiago Bernabéu Stadium, with 70,000 supporters singing his name.

Back to work, he thought. And that was just how he liked it.

DAD THE STRIKER

It was 2008. On a frosty non-league pitch on the outskirts of Birmingham, a battle was taking place. Two men's teams were going head-to-head in a Sunday game. Only a few dozen people were watching, but the players were giving it everything. Their breath fogged in the cold air. Shouts echoed around the pitch. Tackles were flying in.

On the sidelines, two tiny brothers in woolly hats and warm coats looked on with their mum. It was a tight match – 0-0 with five minutes to go – but the boys were desperate for a winner. And they wanted one player in particular to score it.

Then it happened. A goal kick dropped from the sky, bounced off a defender's head and fell towards the centre-forward. He used his strength to shoulder his marker out of the way, then slammed a shot past the keeper. The net bulged.

"Yesss!" yelled his teammates, crowding the scorer. "Get in there, Mark!"

No one was more delighted than the little brothers. Their names were Jude and Jobe, and they were five and three years old. "Yaaayy!" they shouted, doing an excited dance. "Well done, Daddy!"

For the two boys, having a dad who scored goals was something they'd always known. Mark Bellingham worked as a police officer, but he was also a brilliant striker. Every weekend, Jude and Jobe's dad changed his sergeant's uniform for his football kit. Over the past fourteen years, he'd played for nine different non-league clubs and scored hundreds of goals.

At full-time, Mark came over to see his family. The two boys ran up and gave him a hug. "Amazing, Daddy," said Jude, the eldest. "You did it again!"

Mark ruffled his hair. "Thanks, son," he laughed.

"We watched you all game," continued Jude. "You ran and ran and ran. You never stopped trying. That's why your team won."

Mark looked down at him and smiled. The boy was learning fast.

Jude Victor William Bellingham was born on Sunday 29 June, 2003, in the town of Stourbridge, near Birmingham. His parents, Mark and Denise, were kind and hard-working. They lived in a village in the West Midlands called Hagley and and did all they could to help Jude learn the right lessons in life.

From an early age, Denise and Mark taught Jude the importance of good manners and perseverance. They also introduced him to football. Even as a toddler, he was taken to watch his dad play for Bromsgrove Rovers on Sundays. The windy pitches and noisy goal celebrations became part of the little boy's weekly routine.

But young Jude didn't get the football bug straight away. He loved running around on the sidelines and playing chase games, but if a ball rolled his way he would look at it strangely. Instead of kicking it, he would pick it up and throw it!

Then, not long after his fifth birthday, something clicked. As his dad's team warmed up before a Sunday match, Jude wandered on to the pitch and started playing with one of the balls. He took a run-up. "Bang!" he said to himself, swinging his trainer and trying to copy his dad's big shots.

The ball didn't go far, so he kicked it again. Bang! It went further this time. He could see grown-ups watching him and smiling. He ran up to the ball again as fast as he could and – bang! This time the ball went looping into the air. Jude's eyes lit up. Kicking a football was fun.

It was the beginning of an obsession.

As a young boy, Jude was bubbly, energetic and a bit cheeky at times, but big-hearted too. He was kind to his friends and always full of giggles at birthday parties or on family days out.

His dad was his first football hero – he felt proud to be the son of a hotshot striker – but it wasn't until later that he became interested in famous players. For now, he loved the simple joy of playing with a ball: the way it bounced; the way you could run around with it for half an hour and feel out of breath, but still want to carry on; the way it could make you happy.

By now, he wasn't the only boy in the house. His brother Jobe had been born in September 2005. Jobe was less than two years younger than Jude, and just as active. When they were both old enough to kick a ball to each other – well, there was no stopping them.

"Pass it, Jobe, pass it!"

Jude had got home from primary school just minutes earlier, but he and his brother had already grabbed a football and run to the scrap of grass near their house. The two little boys loved everything about football: the dribbling, the heading, the passing, the tackling, the running, the shooting and, of course, the dreaming.

"Bellingham has it," said Jude, pretending to commentate on himself. "He goes past one defender, past two," he continued, weaving around invisible opponents. "And Bellingham SCOOOOOOORES!" he shouted, shooting the ball low into the bushes.

That afternoon, the only spectators they had were a few pigeons. But as the boys kept sprinting and shooting, teasing each other when they got outskilled, anyone watching them could have guessed that they would be used to bigger crowds before too long. Only the thought of a hot meal being cooked at home – baked beans and eggs, Jude's favourite – tore them away from their game.

The staff at Hagley Primary School were used to seeing Jude with a ball at his feet, too. His form teacher Mrs Shackleton noticed him every breaktime and lunchtime, rushing around playing football with his friends.

"He never stops," she said to the PE teacher Mr Ayres, as they noticed Jude charging about the playground one morning. "But what a lovely young boy."

"You're right," replied Mr Ayres. "He's thoughtful and caring with the other children, but full of energy when there's a ball around. He tries hard at cricket, too. A natural little sportsman."

Their conversation turned to other things. A minute later, the school caretaker Mr Williams marched past them with a ladder.

"What's happened, Mr Williams?" asked Mrs Shackleton.

"Can't you guess?" laughed the caretaker. "It's Jude. He's kicked the ball onto the roof again. That's the third time this week!"

THE START OF
THE JOURNEY

Phil Wooldridge was a proud man. Just two years earlier, he'd started running training sessions for local youngsters. His friend Mark Bellingham had helped him with the coaching, and things had gone well.

So well, in fact, that now they had their own brand new Under-7s team, Stourbridge Juniors. Today was their first game. It was a chilly morning, and the youngsters were wearing smart red and white stripes.

"Just go out there, work for each other and enjoy yourselves," said Phil, speaking to the team before kick-off. "That's right," added Mark. "Try your hardest, but make sure you have fun, too."

"Don't worry, Dad," whispered one of the players, as the team ran excitedly onto the pitch. "I will."

When Jude said he was going to have fun, he meant it. He was only six years old, but he bossed the game – running here, dashing there, booting the ball into space for his teammates. After Stourbridge Juniors won 3-0, with Jude scoring two goals, he got back into his parents' car with a huge smile.

"Well done, Jude," said his mum, who had brought Jobe to watch him play. "You tried really hard out there."

"You certainly did," agreed her husband, turning round from the driver's seat. "Keep doing what you're doing, son."

Even Jobe offered congratulations, aiming a kick at his brother's leg across the backseat then giving him a grin. Jude grinned back. "Thanks," he said. Then a terrible thought struck him. "Dad – do we really have to wait a whole week until the next game?"

By now, Jude had discovered more football

heroes. He loved watching England players like Wayne Rooney and Steven Gerrard, and even had his own Lionel Messi replica shirt. In the Bellingham house, if there was a football match on TV, Jude would be in front of the screen, staring, listening and soaking it all up. If there was one thing he loved more than eating baked beans and eggs, it was watching football.

Jude began playing regularly for Stourbridge Juniors, always encouraging his teammates and running from the first whistle to the last. He scored lots of goals with his favourite right foot, but also smashed some in with his left. It was clear he was something special.

His talent didn't remain a secret for long. The Midlands was a football hotspot, and in early 2010 there were four different Premier League clubs within just a few miles of the Bellingham house. Aston Villa, Wolverhampton Wanderers and West Bromwich Albion were three of them. The other was Birmingham City.

One evening, after Jude and Jobe had been out again on the patch of grass with some of their friends, Mark spoke to his eldest son. "You're really enjoying your football, aren't you, Jude?" he smiled. "You're playing out there so often that you're wearing the grass away."

Jude giggled. "I love it, Dad," he said.

"Well, listen," continued Mark. "I've been talking to someone called Simon Jones. He's the head of academy player recruitment at Birmingham City, and he's noticed you. He thinks you've got talent. How would you like to play a few games at the club's pre-academy with other kids your age?"

Jude looked up at his dad. "At Birmingham City? The Blues?" he asked, his eyes widening.

"That's right. What do you think?"

Despite his growing obsession with football, Jude hadn't really thought it was possible that he might get involved with a professional club. Yes, he liked daydreaming that he was a superstar, but surely that was the same for every seven-year-old.

This chat with his dad, however, made his stomach do loop-the-loops. Heading along to play at the Blues academy? Now that sounded like fun.

SCORING FOR FUN

It was two years later, and the defenders from Dudley Town Youth were covered in mud. They were playing Birmingham City Under-10s, whose central midfielder had been running rings around them all afternoon. His dribbling was skilful, his passing was perfect and his speed was incredible.

He'd just scored his fourth goal and there were still twenty minutes to go. He was a blue-shirted, nine-year-old football machine.

"Nice one, Jude!" shouted the player's teammates in delight as he celebrated his latest goal, a curler from outside the box. His midfield partner Noel high-fived him. "Amazing goal, Jude," he said, as the Dudley Town defenders got up from the grass. "We've definitely won this one!"

Jude was getting used to being a match winner. He'd scored dozens of goals for Birmingham City's Under-8s and Under-9s teams, and now he was helping the Under-10s to cruise to victory.

The scariest part – for any defenders, at least – was that he just seemed to be getting better. He still loved messing around with his mates on the grass near his house, but at the academy his skills were really improving.

He always looked forward to training with the coaches, who were helping him understand tactics and teamwork. Most of all, though, he loved playing against other clubs. When he pulled on his Blues shirt, he felt alive.

His mum and dad were there for every game, cheering him on. And not only was Jude flying high for the Under-10s, but Jobe was playing now too – for the academy Under-8s! Denise and Mark were the proudest parents in the Midlands.

Having the Birmingham City badge on his chest meant the world to Jude. The year he'd joined the academy, the men's team had finished ninth in the Premiership, battling hard against the bigger, richer clubs. They didn't have the flashiest squad or the shiniest stadium, but they always played with guts and determination.

The very next season, in fact, they won the Carling Cup, beating Arsenal in front of more than 88,000 fans at Wembley. When Blues striker Obafemi Martins had scored the winner, Jude and Jobe – who were watching on TV – had spent five minutes jumping around the sitting room, yelling with joy.

Jude had even started going to watch matches at St Andrew's, the club's century-old home ground. On a match day, when the floodlights were switched on and the team ran on to the turf, with songs ringing out from the Tilton Road stand, the feeling of excitement was unreal.

St Andrew's had seen some legendary Blues players – people like Trevor Francis, Britain's first ever one-million-pound footballer, and Frank Womack, who played almost five hundred league matches. Then there was Joe Bradford, a forward who had scored two-hundred-and-forty-nine goals for the club. Jude loved hearing stories about them.

Faithful Birmingham City fans are known as Bluenoses. Jude thought the name sounded funny, but he liked it. And there was no doubt about it in his mind – he was now a Bluenose.

He was also now a seriously good goal scorer. So good, in fact, that the academy coaches were realizing he was too skilful for his age.

"I've lost count of how many he's scored today," said coach Mike Dodds to academy manager Kristjaan Speakman, as they stood on a windy touchline, watching Jude wheel away after a neat chip over the keeper.

"That's his fourteenth, and it's not even half-time," replied Kristjaan in amazement.

Just before half-time, Jude raced onto a deep cross. Trapping the ball on his chest, he turned and slammed an overhead kick into the net.

The two coaches looked at each other. "That's it," said Kristjaan. "We've got to move him up a year."

THE BLUENOSE STATUE

Birmingham City fans are known as Bluenoses – and they have their own special statue that honours the nickname. The Sleeping Iron Giant is a large metal sculpture of a sleeping head, on a grassy street-corner near St Andrew's. It was first unveiled in March 1992 – and within months its nose had been painted bright blue by Birmingham City fans!

Today, its nose is still painted blue, and the statue has become so famous with Blues fans that Jude used to insist his mum and dad drove past it every time they took him to a game!

THE NUMBER TWENTY-TWO SHIRT

At first, Jude was sad.

"Do I have to, Dad?" he said, flopping onto the sofa and fiddling with the remote control. "I don't have any mates in the year group above. It won't be fun."

Mark's priority was that Jude kept enjoying his football. He wasn't going to force his son to do something that made him unhappy, but at the same time, he also wanted to give him the best advice.

When he explained to Jude how good it would be to challenge himself, and how he could use his skills to shine, the boy agreed. It was a great decision. Jude scored two on his Under-11s debut against Nottingham Forest and started bonding well with his older teammates.

The coaches were happy. Jude was happy. The journey was continuing.

The Bellingham house was football mad. Mark was a busy policeman, but he still loved playing on Sundays. Each evening, the goalscoring advice would fly around the family dinner table – and not just from Mark.

"You should dink it next time you're through one-on-one, Dad," said Jude, tucking into his spaghetti bolognese.

"Yeah, just to lift it over the keeper's legs," added Jobe.

"I'm not sure," said Mark, thinking about it as he ate. "Bit too risky. Better to choose a corner of the net and shoot hard, I reckon."

Denise smiled to herself and looked around the table. "Right then, football squad. Who wants seconds?"

"Yes, please!" chorused three voices.

As Jude's rise through the academy continued,

the attention around him grew. He seemed to have it all: strength, skill, stamina and speed. He'd helped Hagley Primary get to the national finals – not just for football, but for cricket too. Jude had spent weeks the previous summer working on his cricket skills, desperate to get better, and it had paid off. He'd also represented the school at both cross-country and sprinting.

All this translated into Jude being a superb young midfielder. He was still quite small, but he played with heart and aggression. He was as friendly as a puppy in the changing room, laughing and joking with his friends, but as fierce as a lion when he stepped on to the pitch.

As his performances got even better, it wasn't long before he was moved up yet another year group. This time, though, he wasn't worried. He knew what to do: always give one hundred per cent, never back out of a challenge, keep working, play the right passes and find the right positions.

Simple. At least, that's how Jude made it look.

Within another year, Jude had been shifted all the way up to the Under-14s. He was determined to stay level-headed, but he dreamed of playing for the first team one day.

He'd already seen Demarai Gray, a boy seven years older than him, make the leap from the academy to the matchday squad, and he knew that players like striker Nathan Redmond and goalkeeper Jack Butland had done the same. Jude felt inspired by them. *If they could do it*, he thought, *why can't I?*

One day when the academy players were leaving training, his teammate Tommy ran up to him excitedly. "Jude! Trevor Francis is over there!"

Jude gasped. The former England and Birmingham City legend Trevor Francis – no way! The boys sprinted over to get a photo with him. Back in 1970, Trevor had become the youngest ever Blues player, making his debut aged just sixteen years and one-hundred-and-thirty-nine days. He was friendly and patient when the youngsters ran across, smiling for the camera with them.

Jude was buzzing. He couldn't wait to show his family the picture. And in the meantime, a thought had popped into his head. The youngest ever Blues player? Wow. Just imagine beating the record of the great Trevor Francis…

At the academy, Jude's rise seemed unstoppable. He could tackle, spray passes around and race right through a defence with the ball at his feet. After yet another dazzling display for the Under-14s, Mike Dodds took him to one side.

"Jude, I've been talking with the other coaches," said Mike. "Most midfielders are suited to one main job. They're either defensive midfielders in the number four role, box-to-box midfielders in the number eight role or playmakers in the number ten role." He paused. "But you're all three at the same time!"

Jude's chest swelled. He loved playing for Mike because the coach knew just what to say to keep him motivated. But the youngster wasn't prepared for what came next.

"So we've been thinking," continued Mike. "The total midfielder would be number four plus number eight plus number ten. What does that add up to?"

Jude was confused by the question but did a quick sum. "Twenty-two," he replied.

"Exactly," said Mike, smiling. "So from now on,

that's your shirt number."

Jude loved the idea. Number twenty-two. He could definitely get used to that.

THE LEGENDARY TREVOR FRANCIS

When Jude made his debut for Birmingham City, becoming the club's youngest ever player, he beat the record of one of his heroes, Trevor Francis. Trevor was born in 1954 and made his Blues debut in 1970 against Cardiff City, aged sixteen years and one-hundred-and-thirty-nine days.

After scoring one hundred and nineteen goals for Birmingham, he became the first million-pound player in Britain when he signed for Nottingham Forest in 1979. In the same year, he scored Forest's winning goal in the European Cup final as they beat Swedish side Malmö.

His club career also took him to Manchester City, Sampdoria, Atalanta, Glasgow Rangers, Queens Park Rangers and Sheffield Wednesday. He played fifty-two times for England, scoring twelve goals.

He died in July 2023, aged sixty-nine.

Interviewed in 2020, when Jude was still at Birmingham, Trevor said the following about the Blues' young star: "I'm very, very attracted to what he's doing. He is a player of a young age with great potential and natural ability. But I'm not just looking to see how he performs on a Saturday afternoon or a Wednesday evening. I'm looking at his personality and I'm trying to think how he would cope with some of the things that I had to cope with as a youngster. And it seems to me he's very grounded."

"Sadly, I have to say that many of the youngsters today don't have a lot of time for players who have played the game – they look upon us as has-beens. But Jude shows an interest. I respect him and I really want him to do well. Hopefully he'll go right to the very top."

COUNTRY CALLING

It was the summer of 2016. The Bellingham family had moved to Bromsgrove to be closer to the Blues' training ground, and Jude was now thirteen. He was a pupil at the Priory School in Edgbaston, in Birmingham – and he was more football-obsessed than ever.

Right now, his heart was racing. He had just got in from school and his mum had handed him a letter. The first thing he'd noticed was a small badge printed on the envelope. And not just any badge – a badge showing three lions.

This could only mean one thing.

England.

Breathing hard, he opened it up, unfolded the letter and started reading. Whoaaa! He'd been invited to an England Under-15 training camp. This was crazy!

His mum was smiling. "So, what does it say?" she asked.

Jude could barely speak. "It says... wha... I can't believe it... look!" He beamed and showed his mum the letter, then called to the others, "Dad! Jobe! Come and see!"

A week later he was at a training base in Loughborough, surrounded by confident boys from huge Premier League clubs. There were four from Arsenal, three from Liverpool, four from Manchester City, three from Chelsea, some from Spurs and United – but just one, Jude, from Birmingham City.

He'd had tests before, but never quite like this. For the first time, he started to doubt himself. Was he good enough?

He needn't have worried. As an Under-14, he was the youngest at the camp, but while some of the boys seemed determined to show off in the changing room, Jude stayed quiet and let his feet do the talking: chasing, dribbling, tackling and doing his thing.

From the sideline, Daniel Dodds, the FA's youth talent manager, watched Jude play a forty-yard pass out to the wing. He looked down at his clipboard and checked his birthdate again. The boy had just turned thirteen. "Unbelievable," Daniel whispered to himself.

Jude did enough to be invited back for the next camp a few months later – this time at England's St George's Park.

When he arrived, he gazed at the pitches and the facilities, lost for words. This was where players from England's Euro 2016 squad such as Wayne Rooney, Jordan Henderson, Harry Kane and Raheem Sterling had practised. Whoa!

Only one thing to do, he thought, as the coaches laid out cones on the grass. *Prove that I belong here.*

He did exactly that, playing so well that he was called up to make his Under-15s debut that December against Turkey. He didn't get much game time, but for a youngster like Jude the experience was fantastic. And the feeling of pulling on a fresh white England shirt? It was better than anything.

A few months later, Daniel Dodds and the three other national youth coaches were back in their office, choosing the England Under-15s squad for a match against the Netherlands. Lots of the players from the previous year had moved up to the Under-16s, but not Jude.

"We need a captain," said Daniel, looking down at his player list, which also included upcoming stars like Harvey Elliott, Karamoko Dembélé and Amadou Diallo.

The coaches started thinking. For a captain, they needed a strong, quiet leader, someone popular with the other players but who always played with commitment. Someone with a special talent.

There was a short pause. They looked at each other. Then all four voices said the same name out loud.

"Jude."

FOUR OF JUDE'S ENGLAND YOUTH TEAMMATES

Jamal Musiala

Before switching allegiance to Germany, this fast-dribbling star was part of the England youth set-up. While Jude was at Dortmund, Jamal was playing for their arch-rivals Bayern Munich!

Harvey Elliott

This battling midfielder shot to fame after moving from Fulham to Liverpool, but back in 2019 he was part of Jude's England Under-17s team that won the *Syrenka* Cup. He even scored a goal in the final!

Levi Colwill

Born just four months earlier than Jude, defender Levi was another who came through the England ranks at the same time. He signed for Chelsea in 2020 and made his full England debut in October 2023.

Jarell Quansah

A towering centre-back who became a favourite with Liverpool fans after making his debut in the 2023/24 season, Jarell was another member of England's winning *Syrenka* Cup squad in 2019.

THE PROUDEST BLUE

Captaining his country at youth level – and getting two assists in a strong England performance – was the start of an amazing two years for Jude. At home he was the same boy he'd always been, playing FIFA on the PlayStation, getting his homework done and kicking footballs around with Jobe.

But at the academy, he was flying.

At just fourteen, he'd been fast-tracked up to the Under-18s. "Who's the skinny little kid?" some of the older players had whispered when he arrived for a training game. Ninety minutes and three goals later, they knew exactly who he was.

The same thing happened in October 2018, a few months after Jude's fifteenth birthday, when he was moved up to the Birmingham City Under-23s. Yes, the Under-23s! When he came on as a sub for his debut, he got some funny looks from the opposition. Some even laughed at him. What was this schoolboy doing in the Under-23s team? But when he muscled his way into the box to slide in the winning goal, they weren't laughing anymore.

The coaches knew they had a rare gift on their hands. The very next month, Jude skippered the Birmingham Under-16s in the Blades Cup, helping them beat Manchester United in the semis, then scoring four goals in twenty-two minutes to smash Liverpool 8-4 in the final.

And as if this wasn't enough, Jude then shifted back up to the Under-23s and scored a stunning left-foot curler against Fulham.

Soon, he started being invited to train with the first team. The Blues management were handling Jude well, letting him experience the thrill of the big time – getting him to join warm-ups with the matchday squad and inviting him to travel on the first-team coach – but without overwhelming him.

"Good luck, son!" said Mark, as he and Denise dropped Jude off before another Under-23s game.

They watched their eldest son jog across to join his older teammates. He was tall now. "Look at him, he's really blossoming," said Denise. "It's so easy to forget how young he is," replied Mark. "This club has been the making of him."

By now, other clubs were hearing rumours of a world-class teenager coming out of the Midlands. Scouts were sent to watch him. Arsenal made a transfer bid but were turned down.

Why? Because luckily for Birmingham City, someone else had been wowed by Jude's ability: the Blues' new Spanish manager Pep Clotet.

Pep had decades of experience. He had managed teams in Spain, Sweden and Norway, as well as being an assistant at Leeds United and Swansea City. Now, for the 2019/20 season, he was in the hot seat at the Blues.

And the way Pep saw it, if Jude was good enough to be playing for the first team, then he should be given the chance.

That chance came soon. Pep had already invited him on Birmingham's pre-season tour of Portugal,

38

where Jude was training with experienced pros like Lukas Jutkiewicz, Kristian Pedersen and keeper Lee Camp. Lee was more than twice as old as Jude!

The real opportunity, however, came a couple of weeks later. The Blues had won their opening Championship match against Brentford but Jude hadn't been involved, so when he turned up for the next training session, he wasn't expecting what happened next.

"Okay, we've got an English Football League Cup match at Portsmouth this week," said Pep, speaking to the whole squad. "Great opportunity for us to try something new. Here's the team." He began reading the line-up. "Stockdale in the nets. Defence will be Harding, Bajrami and Clarke-Salter. In midfield we'll have Gardner, Seddon, Delgado, Dacres-Cogley and Lakin. And Crowley up front."

Jude let the names sink in. But hang on, wasn't that only ten players? "Oh, one more," said Pep, winking at the youngster. "Playing behind the striker will be Bellingham."

Jude couldn't believe his ears. Everyone there knew what this meant. Some of the others came over to pat him on the back. He'd blown out the candles on his sixteenth-birthday cake only a few weeks ago. He was about to become the youngest first-team player in the one-hundred-and-forty-four-year history of Birmingham City Football Club.

BIRMINGHAM CITY FC

Nickname: the Blues
Founded: 1875 (The club was first called Small Heath Alliance, then in 1888 became Small Heath, then in 1905 became Birmingham and then in 1943 became Birmingham City!)
Current League: English Championship
Current Manager: Tony Mowbray
Crest: two white spheres, one on top of the other, with a blue ribbon winding around them. The ribbon reads "Birmingham City Football Club 1875". The top sphere is a globe, the bottom sphere is a football.

It was two days later. Fratton Park, Portsmouth's famous old ground, was coated in warm evening sunshine.

Jude tried to look calm as he walked on to the pitch, but his pulse was beating like a drum. The past forty-eight hours had been breathless. When he'd told his family and friends the news, they'd been as excited as he was.

"Yes! Go on, son! You show them what you can do!"

"So proud of you, bro! You're a legend!"

"Jude, mate! That is next level! You'll break Trevor Francis' record!"

"Good lad, Bellers! Amazing!"

His family were there in the stands. But when the whistle went, his mind switched to game mode. This was it. He was now the youngest player in Blues history, at sixteen years and thirty-eight days, and he had a job to do.

A few minutes in, the veteran Portsmouth midfielder Ben Close picked up the ball in midfield. He turned towards goal, but suddenly – crash! A crunching tackle came in from a Birmingham player, winning possession back.

Close didn't know what had hit him. He looked at the player's shirt to see his number.

Twenty-two.

Jude Bellingham had arrived.

AN UNFORGETTABLE SEASON

Things move quickly in the professional game.

If Jude hadn't learned that before now, he was about to. The Blues had lost the Portsmouth game, but Pep and the squad weren't downhearted. The club's priority was the Championship, and the games came thick and fast.

The squad was full of senior players, but Jude had to wait just nineteen days for his next taste of first-team action. This time it was in the league, coming on for fifteen minutes in an away match at Swansea.

Six days later, he was named on the bench again for a home game against Stoke City. More than

20,000 fans had come to St Andrew's to roar on the players, but half an hour in, there was a problem. The Blues winger Jefferson Montero was injured.

Pep looked at his substitutes. Two of them, Dan Crowley and Kerim Mrabti, had already started warming up in expectation. But Pep had other plans.

"Jude," he said. "Get your tracksuit off. You're on."

Jude didn't have time to feel nervous. Suddenly, he was in the action.

He would never forget the moment he first ran on to the St Andrew's pitch, or the noise of the fans as they cheered his arrival.

He would never forget how disappointed he felt when Stoke took the lead in the second half, or how overjoyed he felt when Birmingham equalized a quarter of an hour later.

Most of all, though, he would never forget the seventy-sixth minute.

With fourteen minutes of normal time left, the ball came to him in the Stoke half. Thinking quickly, he turned and started running towards the defenders. For a moment he looked like he would make a pass, and in that split second they backed away. Big mistake.

Jude was twenty-five yards out.

Right, he thought. *Shoot.*

He fizzed his right foot through the ball. He didn't catch it cleanly, but it had pace. The shot clipped a defender, wrong-footing the keeper. Then the world went into slow-motion, and as Jude's head exploded with happiness, the ball rolled gently into the net.

GOOOOAAAALLLLLL!

The stadium erupted. Jude was in wonderland. He screamed at the top of his lungs and sprinted towards the Tilton Stand behind the goal, sliding on his knees. A second later, he was mobbed. His teammates were hugging him. Fans were on the pitch in a frenzy.

Birmingham's youngest ever first-team player? He was now their youngest ever goal scorer, too. And he'd just bagged the winner in a Championship match.

Jude soon became a fixture in the first team. The fans loved his drive and energy, and he was a Bluenose – one of their own! After he scored another winner two weeks later, this time away at Charlton, his performances started attracting Premier League clubs.

"Have you heard about the sixteen-year-old kid at Birmingham City? He's starting week-in, week-out in the Championship. We need to send someone to check him out."

And when Jude travelled out to Poland to captain the England Under-17s in the *Syrenka* Cup, coming back with the trophy, the noise only grew louder.

Now, wherever the Blues went, scouts followed. Pep was using Jude in different positions – sometimes as a box-to-box midfielder, sometimes out wide, sometimes behind the attackers – but he always played well. He ran all game and tackled without fear. At grounds around the country, from Leeds United to Fulham and from Middlesbrough to West Brom, the boy wonder was playing like a man.

Pep knew what to expect in the January transfer window. As soon as it opened, the bids came in from Manchester United and other huge English clubs, but also from clubs in Italy and Germany. They all wanted Jude.

Happily for the Blues, their young star was staying patient. He was also receiving sensible advice from his parents. Even now, they were making sure he didn't fall behind with his schoolwork. "I'm not moving midway through the season, boss," said Jude to Pep. "I want to stay until the summer. This is my club."

A few weeks later, the world was stunned by the outbreak of Covid-19. It was a worrying time, and fixtures were cancelled right across Europe, but Jude tried to stay focused.

When matches restarted, he was playing to empty stadiums. No problem. He gave one hundred per cent every time he wore the shirt, and while it wasn't a glorious season for the Blues, Jude's passion and skill helped them avoid relegation.

In his final match for his boyhood club, Jude lined up at St Andrew's against Derby County. There were no fans in the stands, but who was in midfield for Derby? None other than Wayne Rooney, one of Jude's heroes. *This is like some sort of dream*, thought the youngster, as he jostled with Wayne at a corner.

But the dream was just beginning. Mark and Denise had spent the last few months listening to Jude and discussing what sort of move would be best for him. The Premier League? No. Too much pressure for a sixteen-year-old. Too much spotlight.

They all agreed he'd be better moving overseas, where he could keep improving his game. Together, they'd found the perfect club: a big German team with a long history of developing young players.

Jude was seventeen now. And he was off to Borussia Dortmund.

ALWAYS A BLUE

When his transfer was confirmed, Birmingham City announced that Jude's number twenty-two shirt would be retired.

"In a remarkably short space of time," said the statement. "Jude has become an iconic figure at the Blues, showing what can be achieved through talent, hard work and dedication."

Jude couldn't believe it. What an honour! He felt emotional when he went into the training ground to say goodbye to the coaches and teammates who had been at his side for almost a decade.

He headed straight for Mike Dodds, to thank

the coach who had helped him through so many youth games. "I'm proud of you," said Mike. "Not just for the player you've become, but the person you've become."

"Thanks for everything, Mike," said Jude, trying not to well up.

He said dozens of goodbyes that afternoon, reliving the years he'd spent at the club. He'd been a tiny seven-year-old when he joined the pre-academy. Now he was almost an adult. When he left, he stopped to have a final word with Mike and Kristjaan.

"I might be back one day," smiled Jude. "You know what they say, 'Once a blue, always a blue.'"

As the coaches watched the seventeen-year-old walk away from the training ground, they felt a mixture of happiness and sadness. "Know what I think?" said Kristjaan, as Jude wandered into the distance. "We've learned as much from him as he has from us."

A NEW HERO FOR DORTMUND

In July 2020, a plane touched down in Germany carrying Borussia Dortmund's new seventeen-year-old signing.

"Jude," said the man who had been sent to meet him. "Welcome to Dortmund."

His first day in Germany was a busy one. He met some of the coaching staff, who handed him his new yellow training kit, then got driven to Dortmund's enormous stadium. The famous *Westfalenstadion* was empty, but Jude had goosebumps from just standing on the turf.

Outside Covid-19, the stands here held 80,000

fans on a match day. Jude felt butterflies in his stomach. If he was looking for the big time, he'd found it.

Things got even more exciting when he met his teammates at training. They were serious, trophy-winning pros – he'd watched most of them playing Champions League games on TV. Over there were World Cup stars Mats Hummels, Marco Reus and Axel Witsel. Warming up next to them were speedy youngsters Jadon Sancho and Gio Reyna. *Playing here is going to be seriously fun*, thought Jude, heading across to join them.

Then, as he started a passing drill with Gio, he noticed a tall blond player smashing a ball into the net from thirty yards out. Whoa! What a strike!

The player jogged over to introduce himself. "Hi Jude," he said, grinning. "I'm Erling Haaland."

Jude wasn't out in Germany alone. When his move was agreed, the Bellingham family had sat down to discuss their plans. Jobe was still doing well at the Blues academy, and although Mark had recently retired from football – after scoring more than seven-hundred non-league goals – he was still working as a police sergeant.

The solution was agreed. Mark would stay in England with Jobe. "And I'll come out to Dortmund with you," said Denise to Jude.

The news was a relief. His family had always been his rock, and having his mum close by would be just the support he needed. He'd only just turned seventeen, after all. And as an added bonus, she also cooked the best baked beans and eggs in the world. Even athletes like Jude needed the occasional treat for dinner.

Luckily, though, his mum wasn't there when he was asked to sing in front of the rest of the Dortmund squad. It was a club tradition that all new players had to choose one of their favourite songs to perform. Nervous, but keen to show he was part of the team, Jude stood on a chair at the training ground and brought up the lyrics to 'So Sick' by Ne-Yo on his phone. Then he sang.

Within seconds, his new teammates were doubled over with laughter. This young kid had courage, that was for sure. He was humble, and he had a right foot like a rocket, but, oh boy, his voice was terrible.

They cheered him when he finished, but Jadon couldn't control his giggles. Being English speakers, he and Jude had bonded already. "Oh, mate," he said, wiping his eyes as he spoke to his new friend. "It's lucky you became a footballer. You'd be the world's worst singer!"

Jude's official debut came in mid-September, in the *DFB-Pokal Cup*. Dortmund were playing away at Duisburg. Covid-19 meant the stadium was almost empty, but the match felt huge to Jude. He wanted to show what he could do.

His chance arrived in the first half. Jadon had already put them 1-0 up from the penalty spot, and in the thirtieth minute Dortmund broke forward again. After some lovely work from Gio, the ball fell to Thorgan Hazard at the edge of the box. Thorgan looked up, then heard a call behind him.

"Yes – I'm in space!"

Instantly, Thorgan backheeled it… and there was Jude, rushing on to the pass. He took one touch, then side-footed it hard towards the goal. The ball flicked off the keeper's legs and went bouncing into the net.

GOOOOAAAALLLL!

Jude pointed to his yellow number-twenty-two shirt as he celebrated with the other players. He couldn't hide his delight. Dortmund had spent twenty-five million pounds to bring him across from England, and he was up and running already. What was more, he'd just become the club's youngest ever goal scorer!

Five days later, he made his home debut in the season's first league match, against Borussia Mönchengladbach. He played a clever pass to Gio for the opening goal, which was followed by two from Erling. There were just 10,000 fans allowed in the stands, but they never stopped singing. A 3-0 win at the *Westfalenstadion* in his first ever *Bundesliga* match? *Yes, please*, thought Jude. *I'll take that!*

In training, he treated each practice match like a challenge, desperate to match the quality of his teammates. He was brave when he had possession and even braver when he was tackling. It was a step up from playing with the Blues, but he gave each session everything he had.

At the end of the month, his new boss, Lucien Favre, took him to one side. Jude had just spent half an hour working on his finishing, slamming shots past keeper Roman Bürki. "You must be exhausted, Jude," laughed the manager. "You show more intensity in training than most players show in matches!"

Jude was thrilled that he'd noticed.

"And I've got some good news," continued Lucien.

"You've just been named the *Bundesliga*'s Rookie of the Month."

He patted the youngster on the back and walked away. "Congratulations! Keep up the good work."

Jude smiled and started shooting again. Keeping up the good work was very much his plan.

BORUSSIA DORTMUND

Nicknames: the Black and Yellows, the BVB
Founded: December 1909
Current League: German *Bundesliga*
Current Manager: Edin Terzić
Crest: a yellow circle with black trim, with the letters BVB and the numbers zero and nine (BVB is short for *Ballspiel-Verein* Borussia Dortmund, the club's name; the numbers show the date the club was founded)

FINDING HIS FEET

In the 2020/21 season, Dortmund had one of the most exciting teams in Europe. Jude was playing with top internationals and world-class youngsters. Gio was a fast dribbler and a battling midfielder, only eight months older than Jude. Jadon was a twenty-year-old winger who had already played over a hundred times for the club. And Erling? He was only twenty, too. Jude had never played with a striker with so much natural talent.

Jude was working hard with his training, but he was also working hard off the pitch. Denise made sure of that. He was taking three German lessons a week as well as keeping up-to-date with his college diplomas. "You've got to look after your future," his mum reminded him, as he settled down to more coursework.

Some youngsters might have complained, but not Jude. He still had time to chill in his city-centre apartment, or play FIFA with Gio and Jadon. And whenever it was time to step on to the pitch for Dortmund, he felt like the luckiest person alive.

In mid-October he made his first ever Champions League start, away in Italy against Lazio. The Champions League! Jude was thrilled as the anthem echoed around Rome's Olympic Stadium before kick-off. Dortmund lost 3-1, but Jude had become the youngest ever Englishman to play in the tournament. Yet another record!

A few weeks later, when he was relaxing in his apartment, his phone rang. It was a number from the UK, but not one he recognized.

"Hello?" he said.

"Jude," said the voice at the other end. "It's Gareth Southgate here."

He sat bolt upright. The England manager! What was going on?

Gareth explained that some of the senior squad had picked up injuries, and that they needed players to replace them. There was a friendly against Ireland coming up.

"So," said Gareth. "Would you like to join the squad?"

"Would I? I'd love to!" replied Jude. His smile could almost be heard down the phone line.

Days later, he was back at St George's Park, this time training as a senior player. Feeling starstruck, he introduced himself to his fellow squad members, who included Harry Kane, Jordan Pickford, Jordan Henderson, Jack Grealish and Raheem Sterling. Wow! And he was delighted to see a familiar face coming over to greet him.

"Bro," said Jadon, beaming. "You deserve this."

The next night at Wembley, Jude was named on the bench. He thought that would be the best thing about the evening, but after England cruised into a 3-0 lead, Gareth looked to his subs.

Mason Mount was taken off – and on came Jude!

His first touches were nervy, but by full-time he was passing with his usual flair. He played like he belonged there. The stands were still empty, but Gareth applauded him at the final whistle. His senior international debut – at seventeen!

That night, in his hotel, the last thing he looked at before turning off his light was a shirt draped across his chair. A men's England shirt. And on the back, the name Bellingham.

He was soon in yellow again. For Dortmund, the big matches kept coming. They were finding their rhythm in the Champions League, hitting three past Club Brugge, holding Lazio to a draw, then beating Zenit St Petersburg in Russia. "We've topped our group!" said Gio, high-fiving Jude as they walked back down the tunnel. "Into the last sixteen!"

Things were going well in the *Bundesliga*, too. Edin Terzić had taken over from Lucien Favre as manager, and he'd energized the squad. They were winning matches in the league and seemed to be unbeatable in the *DFB-Pokal Cup*.

Jude had to admit that he found it strange playing in empty stadiums, but for the millions watching Dortmund's matches on TV, the seventeen-year-old was becoming a legend. The social media messages came flooding in.

"The Yellow Army loves you, Jude!"

"We're so happy to have you at Dortmund!"

"Keep going, Jude! You play like a young warrior!"

For Jude and his teammates, the season was building to two big moments. The first came in the Champions League in April, after a win against Sevilla set up a quarter-final against Manchester City. They lost the first leg in Manchester 2-1 – but how would they get on in the second leg at Dortmund?

Jude was going to do everything he could to win. He looked at the City players as they lined up. With stars like Kevin de Bruyne, Bernardo Silva and Rodri, they were going to be hard to beat. *Maybe, though*, thought Jude. *Just maybe.*

Fourteen minutes in, Erling broke down the left for Dortmund. He laid the ball off to Mahmoud Dahoud, who shot first time. The ball hit a defender and bounced towards Jude on the edge of the box. It was now or never. He took two quick touches and sent a bending shot high towards the top corner. Would Ederson save it? No! The shot was too good!

GOOOOOAAALLLL!

Dortmund were level on aggregrate – they'd

evened out the score over the two matches – and Jude had got his first ever Champions League goal! For the rest of the half, he and his teammates chased and harried, determined to take the lead. But in the second half City pressed hard, scoring twice through Riyad Mahrez and Phil Foden. There was no way back. As the final whistle echoed around the ground, the *Westfalenstadion* felt emptier than ever.

"We'll learn from this," said Edin to his players, as Jude kicked off his boots in frustration. "We've got the *DFB-Pokal Cup* semi-final against Holstein Kiel coming up. Let's bounce back."

Outside in the interview room, City boss Pep Guardiola was full of praise when he was asked about Jude. "I can't believe it – maybe he's a liar!" said Pep. "He's so good for seventeen years old."

The words boosted Jude. And sure enough, when Dortmund won their *DFB-Pokal Cup* semi – with goals that included a long-range drive from Jude – they were faced with the season's second huge moment. They would be playing RB Leipzig in the final of Germany's biggest cup competition, at Berlin's Olympic Stadium.

When the big night arrived, the players were

ready. They knew that millions of Dortmund fans would be tuning in on TV. Jude had been receiving good-luck messages all week.

"I know we can do this," said Jadon to Erling and Jude, as they warmed up on the pitch.

"Leipzig finished ahead of us in the *Bundesliga*," replied Erling, stretching his calf muscles. "But we can definitely beat them."

Jude nodded and concentrated on his pre-match routine. Winning a major honour would be incredible.

Sure enough, Dortmund's young heroes played their hearts out. Just five minutes in, Jadon got them off to a flying start with a sweet strike past the keeper. 1-0! Then Erling joined in the fun, muscling away his marker and slotting home. 2-0! When Jadon scored again before half-time, they were in dreamland. 3-0!

There was just one downside for Jude. His excitement had seen him booked for a heavy tackle. Edin had a hard decision to make at half-time. "I'm taking you off," he told his young midfielder. "We can't risk a red card."

Jude was disappointed, but he understood. He

still had things to learn, he knew that. But on the plus side, he got to watch his teammates closing out the match 4-1. Dortmund had won the German Cup. Yes! As he joined the other players to hoist the golden trophy into the air, he looked into the night sky and whooped for joy.

The boy from Hagley was still a month away from his eighteenth birthday – and he now had a major honour to his name.

THE ROAR OF
THE CROWD

The noise was like the storm to end all storms.

It was October 2021. Jude had already played more than fifty times for Dortmund, but today, lining up for kick-off in a *Bundesliga* match against Mainz, his heart was soaring. He and his teammates had played in predominantly empty grounds during the Covid-19 pandemic. Now, for the first time since his move, more than 60,000 fans had been allowed into *Westfalenstadion*.

The stadium was now a huge yellow cauldron. Flags were being waved, drums were being thumped, scarves were being held aloft. Chants were booming from everywhere, but Jude couldn't stop staring at the south stand behind the goal. It was one of the largest grandstands in the whole of Europe. It went up, and up, and up, packing in tens of thousands of fans.

People had a nickname for it. The Yellow Wall. Right now, it looked like a giant carnival and sounded like rolling thunder. He turned to look at Erling. "Wow," they mouthed to each other. Jude felt the hairs on the back of his neck standing up. Playing for Dortmund was one thing, but playing in an atmosphere like this was something else.

The past few months had been unforgettable. Shortly after the *DFB-Pokal Cup* final, he'd been named the *Bundesliga*'s Newcomer of the Season by his fellow players. Then he'd been picked as a back-up midfielder in England's squad for the Euros, making three substitute appearances as the Three Lions made it all the way to the final. Plus, he'd celebrated his eighteenth birthday halfway through the tournament!

Just being part of the England set-up had been a huge achievement for Jude. It showed him how much Gareth Southgate trusted him. It also made him hungrier than ever to become one of England's first-choice midfielders.

Now, back in Germany, he was playing brilliantly. Jadon had left over the summer to join Manchester United for eighty-five million pounds. Jude had been sad to see his friend go, but he didn't let it show on the pitch. Dortmund were flying high in the league and Jude's reputation was growing all the time. A week after the match against Mainz – which Dortmund won 3-1 – he was back in action, away at Bielefeld.

The team were already 2-0 up when the ball came to Jude on the left-hand corner of the box. What followed was football poetry. Shaping to shoot, he instead veered left past one defender, twisted right to get away from another, then turned left again past a third. Through on goal, he lifted the ball coolly over the keeper and across the line.

What a goal! 3-0!

He stretched out his arms and celebrated in front of the travelling Dortmund fans, who were going wild. No one was surprised when the strike was later named the *Bundesliga*'s goal of the month.

As the weeks went by, Jude worked harder than

ever. "You're the key to this team," his skipper Marco told him quietly after training one day. "Just keep believing. Keep your attitude positive, keep learning and keep maturing."

Marco's kind words reminded Jude of the guidance his mum and dad had always given him. He'd come a long way from Stourbridge Juniors, but he knew it was still vital to listen to the right people. And if the great Marco Reus was giving him advice, he was going to follow it. Keep learning. Keep believing.

Off the pitch, Jude was fast becoming one of the most famous footballers in Germany. Fans mobbed him outside the training ground, kids ran up for selfies when he was shopping and his social media feeds were always full of messages from fans.

"Keep your feet on the ground, Jude," said his dad on the phone one night. "We're so proud of you."

"Thanks, Dad," replied Jude. "I've never been in a team that suits me so well."

Two weeks later, it was Jude's turn to be proud. His mobile was buzzing with the news: sixteen-year-old Jobe had made his debut for the Blues first team – aged just sixty-nine days older than Jude had been!

"Little bro!" said Jude, calling to congratulate him. "Those after-school games on the grass paid off for both of us! Thanks for not breaking my record, by the way," he joked.

For Dortmund, it was a season of mixed fortunes. They struggled in the cup competitions, crashing out of both the *DFB-Pokal Cup* and the Champions League, but were still playing heroically in the *Bundesliga*. With Erling, Jude, Axel and Marco linking well together – backed up by players like Raphaël Guerreiro, Manuel Akanji and Julian Brandt – the wins were stacking up.

There was one problem. Their main rivals for the title were the mighty Bayern Munich, and no matter how well Dortmund played, Bayern and their star striker Robert Lewandowski always seemed one step ahead.

After the two clubs played each other near the end of the season – a match which Bayern won 3-1 in front of 75,000 fans – there was no way back for Jude and Dortmund. They finished second in the league.

Jude finished the season with six goals in forty-four appearances and was named in the *Bundesliga's*

Team of the Season. "Not bad for a kid," teased Erling, digging Jude in the ribs and making them both laugh.

But things were changing at Dortmund. While Jude enjoyed a much-needed family summer holiday, with swimming pools and sunshine, Erling signed for Manchester City. Manuel was bought by City, too, and Axel transferred to Atlético Madrid.

So, who would be Dortmund's shining star now?

A WINTER WORLD CUP

Jude knew there were big clubs outside Germany that wanted to sign him. His name was being linked with Chelsea and Liverpool, among others. For now, however, he had a Dortmund badge on his chest and a special few months ahead of him.

Why were they special? There were many reasons. He scored in four Champions League games in a row; he became the *Bundesliga*'s youngest ever captain after wearing the armband for Dortmund against FC Köln; then scored two crackers against Stuttgart at a deafening *Westfalenstadion*. And all this before the end of October!

"You deserve everything that's happening," Edin told him. "This is all down to your hard work. Well done, Jude!"

But there would be even more drama before the end of 2022. This year, for the first time ever, the World Cup was being held in the winter, in Qatar. Jude was nervous before the squads were announced, but he needn't have worried. "Our midfielders will be as follows," said Gareth Southgate on TV, "Gallagher, Henderson, Rice, Phillips, Mount and Bellingham."

"I'm going to Qatar!" Jude said excitedly to his mum, as his phone began beeping with hundreds of alerts. He'd experienced some amazing moments in his career, but this was the biggest stage of all.

Half an hour into England's opening group game against Iran, the fans were getting anxious. Jude had been picked as a starting midfielder and the Three Lions were desperate to start the tournament with a win – but they were being held.

The noisy stands were full of St George's flags and the air was thick with heat. "Come on, England!" screamed the supporters.

Then, after thirty-five minutes, a breakthrough:

Raheem Sterling played a pass to Luke Shaw on the left wing. Looking up, Luke sent a high cross into the box. Jude watched the ball like a hawk, trying to time his run just right.

As he leapt in the air to head it, the world seemed to slow again.

This is your moment, Jude, he told himself.

He met the ball perfectly, using his head to guide the ball over the keeper and into the net. The stadium exploded with noise. GOOOOOOOAAAAALLLLLLLL!

"Yesssss!" shouted captain, Harry Kane, rushing over to celebrate with him.

Jude was in seventh heaven. He'd scored his first England goal – and in the World Cup! He thought about the fans back home and the millions of people who would be watching around the world. He thought about the coaches at Birmingham and Dortmund who had taught him so much, and his family in the stands. What a moment!

Jude's goal opened the floodgates. By full-time, England had won 6-2, setting themselves up perfectly for the rest of their group games. "Another dream come true," he wrote on social media. "Let's keep pushing!"

The following game against the USA, however, was much harder work. Jude and his midfield partner, Declan Rice, ran their socks off in front of nearly 70,000 fans on a hot, sticky night, but England could only manage a 0-0 draw. "Don't let your heads drop, boys!" said Gareth afterwards. "Stay positive!"

To be sure of going through to the next round, they needed a big win in their final group match against Wales. Jude put in a lion-hearted performance, and after two goals from Marcus Rashford and another from Phil Foden, England won 3-0! They were in the last sixteen, where they were up against Senegal.

"This is going to be a tough match," said Bukayo Saka to Jude, as they warmed up. "Senegal have got some big players."

"You're right, mate," replied Jude, looking across at their green-shirted opponents. "We need to be switched on."

This positive attitude brought dazzling rewards. After thirty-nine minutes, shortly after a stunning Jordan Pickford save, Harry Kane collected the ball near the halfway line. Spotting an opportunity, he played a clever through-ball to Jude, who was bursting free down the left. Was this England's big chance?

Jude stayed calm, and with three defenders around him he slotted an inch-perfect ball into the box. There was Jordan Henderson to slot it home!

GOOOOOOALLLL! Jude crouched down and yelled in celebration. The fans in the stands were jumping and screaming. Gareth was on his feet, pumping his fists. 1-0!

The fans made even more noise when Harry scored just before half-time, following some brilliant build-up play from Jude and Phil. And when Bukayo grabbed a third in the second half, it was party time!

A song started thundering around the stadium. "It's coming home, it's coming home, it's coming… football's coming home!"

England were on their way to the World Cup quarter-finals!

HEARTBREAK AND EXCITEMENT

After the Senegal game, Jude's teammates were full of praise for him. "He has no weakness in his game," Harry told the media. "He's incredible – a one-off," added Jordan. Phil went even further, telling journalists that he thought Jude "will be the best midfielder in the world".

But Jude and England had a huge challenge ahead. Their quarter-final opponents were France, the current world champions, who had Kylian Mbappé up front.

It was the biggest match of Jude's career. He was nineteen now, standing over six feet tall and still getting stronger. He knew that England had enough quality players to beat France – but would they perform on the night?

"Let's do this!" shouted Harry, as the team walked out of the tunnel. The national anthems echoed into the sky, sung by tens of thousands of voices. Jude looked around at his teammates and felt filled with hope. Bukayo, Harry, Phil, Declan – they were all born to be winners. Game time.

It was seventeen minutes in when things went wrong, as a long-range strike from French midfielder Aurélien Tchouaméni put France ahead. England were still one down at half-time. "Let's be patient," said Gareth in the dressing room. "Keep calm, keep pressing. We can do this!"

Less than two minutes into the second half, the ball bounced to Jude on the edge of the box. He knew what he had to do. Connecting sweetly with his right foot, he sent a speeding volley towards the goal. Was this 1-1? No! Tipped over by the keeper!

There was better news five minutes later. Jude laid the ball off to Bukayo, who made a mazy run into the area before being cut down. Penalty, surely? Yes! And Harry made no mistake from the spot.

England were level!

The match became tense. Both sides knew that the next goal would be crucial. Harry Maguire went close with a header for England; Olivier Giroud nearly scored with a volley for France. The noise of the fans was deafening.

But on seventy-eight minutes, it was Giroud who finally found the net, nodding a header past Jordan Pickford. France were 2-1 up. Was it game over?

Not if Jude had anything to do with it. Collecting the ball in midfield two minutes later, he looked up to see Mason Mount making a run into the box. Jude's lofted pass had to be perfect – and it was. But just as Mason was about to reach it, he was barged to the ground! Another penalty!

Jude and his teammates were euphoric. If they got it back to 2-2, they knew they could go on and win. The semi-final was in touching distance! They just needed Captain Harry to score again. He would, wouldn't he?

The ball was on the spot. Harry was ready. As millions of England fans 3,500 miles away watched their TV screens through their fingers, he gave a short run-up... and sent the ball ballooning over the bar.

At full-time, Jude, Harry and the rest of the team

were crushed. They were exhausted and soaked in sweat. Their World Cup dream was over.

"I'm so proud of the effort, fight and performance from my teammates," wrote Jude on social media the next day. "Thank you to the fans for the love and support. Keep the faith – our time will come."

Borussia Dortmund's dynamic young midfielder was now in the spotlight. His performances at the World Cup had impressed everyone. Now, it seemed like almost every big club on the planet wanted to sign him: Liverpool and Chelsea, sure, but also Manchester City and Paris Saint Germain, among others.

Leading the race for his signature, however, was the most successful European club of all time: the unstoppable Real Madrid. Would they get their man?

Back in Germany, Jude tried to stay focused on the rest of the season. He couldn't stop Dortmund losing to Chelsea in the last sixteen of the Champions League, but he made sure they kept up the pressure on Bayern Munich at the top of the *Bundesliga*. From late January to mid-March, they won eight games in a row.

At every training session, the coaches and senior players kept the squad feeling positive. Jude, too, was now one of the loudest in the squad. He was nineteen, but he had the mindset of a senior player. "This can be our season!" he told his teammates. "Let's do it for the fans!"

At every home game, the Yellow Wall roared out songs to help the team. They were playing like heroes. When the final match of the season came around, Dortmund were two points ahead of Bayern in second. If Dortmund won at home to Mainz, they would be champions!

But on the day of the game: disaster! Jude had a knee problem that kept him on the bench. He could only watch as Dortmund went 2-0 down. And despite dragging the match back to 2-2 in front of 80,000 nervous fans, it wasn't enough to win the title. Bayern had won the Bundesliga again.

Jude was distraught. He walked on to the pitch with tears in his eyes, applauding the fans. Even the fact that he'd been named the *Bundesliga* Player of the Season couldn't cheer him up.

Back in the dressing room, as the Dortmund players slumped on the benches, Jude began the painful process of saying goodbye to his teammates. He knew he had played his last game for the club that had given him so many magical memories.

"Bye, Jude," said Marco. "You've got a bright future. Thank you for everything."

The summer break would be a short one. But once Jude got over the bitter disappointment of missing out on the title in Dortmund, it would also be an exciting one.

Why?

The boy from the West Midlands was off to Real Madrid.

REAL MADRID CLUB DE FÚTBOL

Nicknames: los Blancos (the Whites), los Merengues (the Meringues)
Founded: March 1902
Current League: *La Liga*
Current Manager: Carlo Ancelotti
Crest: a yellow circle topped by a royal crown. Within the circle, the letters M, C and F (for Madrid Club de Fútbol) appear over a white and blue pattern.

LA LIGA'S NEW MEGASTAR

"This is the proudest day of my life," said Jude, speaking to a packed TV press conference at Real Madrid's Santiago Bernabéu Stadium. He had now officially signed for the club, for one-hundred-and-fifteen million pounds. "It's the day I join the greatest team in the history of the game."

"Thank you to everyone," he said, then looked down at Mark, Denise and Jobe, who had travelled there together to be in the front row. "But, most importantly, to my family for all their support."

Jude still couldn't quite believe where he was. The sense of history at the Bernabéu was immense.

Real had won the European Cup and Champions League a record fourteen times, more than twice as many as their nearest rival. They'd won *La Liga* thirty-five times and the FIFA Club World Cup five times. They'd had players as great as Alfredo Di Stéfano, Cristiano Ronaldo and Zinedine Zidane.

Now Jude was part of that history – and he'd been given the number five shirt made famous by Zidane. It was like being in a fantasy film.

This feeling continued when he met his new teammates. His fellow midfielders were Croatian wizard Luka Modrić, German superstar Toni Kroos, Uruguayan maestro Fede Valverde and two brilliant French players from the World Cup, Aurélien Tchouaméni and Eduardo Camavinga. Also in the squad were rock-solid defenders Éder Militão and Antonio Rüdiger and flying forwards Vinícius Júnior, Joselu and Rodrygo. Just wow. Jude was surrounded by some of the top footballers on Earth.

And the manager? He was pretty decent, too.

"Welcome to Real Madrid," smiled Carlo Ancelotti at Jude's first training session. Carlo was one of the most respected managers in the game, with four Champions League trophies to his name.

He looked Jude in the eyes. "I've worked with thousands of different players," he said. "But very few have been as good as you. With this team, and with you, we can make magic happen."

The next two months were a whirlwind. Away from football, Jude was busy settling into the city. He was enjoying the sunshine, learning Spanish and having meals cooked for him in his house by a personal chef.

On the pitch, meanwhile, he was quickly becoming a global sensation.

He scored five times in his first four *La Liga* games: a bouncing volley against Athletic Bilbao, two quick-thinking goals against Almería, a diving header against Celta and a ninety-fifth-minute tap-in winner against Getafe.

His new teammates called him Belli. The fans called him a miracle. Carlo was right – magic was happening.

When they played Osasuna in early October, the Bernabéu was filled with 70,000 fans. The volume was incredible. Looking around him before kick-off, Jude saw countless shirts and scarves with his name on. Was this really happening? It was.

As the whistle blew, a familiar thought came to his head. His dad's old advice: keep doing what you're doing.

It took only nine minutes for the magic to continue. Luka slid a ball through to Dani Carvajal, who knocked it back to Jude. Racing into the box, he took two quick touches then slammed the ball high into the net. GOAAAAALLLLLLLLL!

He ran across to do his usual celebration in front of the cheering crowd: feet apart, arms out wide, head nodding. Another beautiful goal from the young English megastar.

"Yes, Belli!" said Vinícius Júnior, rushing over to hug him.

On fifty-three minutes, he had another chance. Cutting in from the left, he played a neat one-two with Fede and found himself through on goal. The volume in the stadium went crazy. Would he score? Of course he would! A calm shot through the keeper's legs – 2-0!

As he celebrated again, the stadium trembled with chanting. "LAAAA-LA-LA, LA-LA-LA-LA! LA-LA-LA-LA! HEY, JUDE!"

By full-time, Real had won 4-0 and Jude had now scored ten goals in all competitions for Los Blancos. Later, he summed it up perfectly on social media: "Beautiful win at the temple. Double figures."

For Jude, life in Madrid was amazing. His mum – his "queen", as he called her – was here with him, but he also loved going out into the city with his new friends like Vinícius Júnior, Éder and Brahim Díaz. Everywhere he went, he signed autographs and posed for selfies. His dad regularly visited him too. Jobe came over when he could, but he was much busier these days – he was now a Sunderland player!

Jude's focus was here in Spain. The last *La Liga* match of October was a giant one. He had been looking forward to it for weeks. Real were playing away at Barcelona, their arch-rivals. *El Clásico*. The world would be watching.

It was a sunny, cloudless afternoon. The sold-out stadium was rocking with Barça songs at kick-off, and when İlkay Gündoğan put the hosts ahead after nine minutes, the noise was intense.

Things stayed that way until the sixty-eighth minute. There were good chances at both ends, but no one could find the net. Then a clearing Barça header fell to Jude forty yards out. He controlled the ball and, as defenders closed in, he looked up.

Right, he thought. *It's showtime.*

Powering his right foot through the ball, he fired a thunderbolt of a shot into the top corner. GOOOOOAAAAAAALLLLL!

It was a glorious strike, one of his best ever – but he wasn't done yet.

As the match ticked into added time, with the score at 1-1, Real broke down the right. Dani sent in a low cross, which Luka touched on towards the goal. And who was there to knock it home with a right-foot finish?

GOOOOOAAAAAAALLLLL! Jude had got the winner in *El Clásico*!

The away fans were jumping all over each other in delight. Jude stood there in front of them with his arms outstretched.

This is a fairytale, he thought, as the TV commentators went crazy and Dani and Luka ran over to leap on his back. From Hagley Primary School to *El Clásico. Not bad,* he said to himself, smiling widely. *Not bad at all.*

SUPER CUP STAR

In 2024, ten weeks after picking up the Kopa Trophy at the *Ballon d'Or* ceremony in Paris, Jude had the chance to win his first silverware with Real Madrid.

They were playing in the Spanish Super Cup final, which was being held in Saudi Arabia. And their opponents? Who else? Barcelona!

Thanks to Jude's superstar performances, Real were having a brilliant season in *La Liga* and had already reached the knock-out stages of the Champions League. Winning the Super Cup would be just what they needed to spur them on.

Typically, it was Jude who got things started,

playing a brilliant through-ball to Vinícius Júnior in the seventh minute. 1-0! Viní scored again three minutes later, then converted a penalty before half-time. Robert Lewandowski had got one back for Barça, but when Rodrygo scored Real's fourth in the second half, it was game over. 4-1!

The players and Carlo paraded the trophy around the ground after the game, dancing under the night sky as the fans applauded. Jude looked at the gleaming cup, then at his teammates. What stars they were! Fede, Brahim, Rodrygo, Dani, Vinícius Júnior, Éder, Toni, Luka – he felt a bond with them all.

On social media, he posted four photos from the celebrations. Above them, he wrote the words: "First trophy with the greatest club in the world! HALA MADRID!"

There would be many years ahead for Jude, his teammates, his fans and his family – and one thing was for sure. He'd come a long way already, and this wouldn't be his last celebration for club and country.

Bellingham's Timeline

29 June 2003   Jude is born to parents Denise and Mark in Wordsley Hospital, Stourbridge.

23 September 2005   His younger brother, Jobe, is born, also in Stourbridge.

2010   While Jude is a seven-year-old pupil at Hagley Primary School, he is invited to join the Birmingham City FC academy.

2016   Aged thirteen, Jude is called up to join an Under-15s training camp for England. He impresses and is called back to train at St George's Park, making his Under-15s debut against Turkey in December.

2017	Having risen rapidly through the Birmingham ranks, a fourteen-year-old Jude makes his first appearance for the Blues Under-18s.
15 October 2018	Aged fifteen, he makes his debut for the Birmingham City Under-23s.
6 November 2018	As captain, he helps the Blues Under-17s win the Blades Cup, beating Liverpool 8-4 in the final. Jude gets four of the goals.
6 August 2019	Jude makes his first-team debut for the Blues, starting in an EFL Cup match against Portsmouth. At sixteen years and thirty-eight days, he is the youngest player ever to play for the club.
25 August 2019	Jude comes on as a substitute in an away game at Swansea City, making his league debut.

31 August 2019	Jude comes off the bench and grabs the winner against Stoke City, becoming the Blues' youngest ever scorer on his home debut.
10 September 2019	Jude captains the England Under-17s to victory in the *Syrenka* Cup in Poland, beating the hosts 3-1 on penalties. Jude is named Player of the Tournament.
20 July 2020	It is confirmed that Jude will join Borussia Dortmund at the end of the season for twenty-five million pounds.
22 July 2020	He makes his last appearance for Birmingham City, in a match against Derby County. His performances over the season help the Blues to avoid relegation by two points.

14 September 2020	Jude makes his debut for Dortmund, against Duisburg in the *DFB-Pokal Cup*. He gets the second goal in a 5-0 win, becoming the club's youngest ever scorer.
20 October 2020	He starts against Lazio in the Champions League, becoming the youngest ever Englishman to play in Europe's top club tournament.
12 November 2020	Having been called up to the senior England squad for the first time, he makes his debut as a substitute against Ireland at Wembley.
10 April 2021	He scores his first *Bundesliga* goal in a 3-2 win over Stuttgart.
14 April 2021	He scores his first Champions League goal in a 2-1 defeat against Manchester City.

13 May 2021	Jude helps Dortmund to beat RB Leipzig 4-1 in the final of the *DFB-Pokal Cup*, Germany's biggest cup competition.
June 2021	Jude is named in the England squad for the delayed Euro 2020 tournament. When he comes on as a substitute against Croatia on 13 June, aged seventeen years and three-hundred-and-forty-nine days, he becomes England's youngest ever player at a major tournament.
May 2022	With Jude's help, Dortmund finish second in the *Bundesliga*, eight points behind Bayern Munich.
November 2022	Jude is named in the England squad for the FIFA World Cup in Qatar. He gets his first senior goal for his country in a 6-2 win over Iran in England's opening match, on 21 November.

10 December 2022	Despite performing admirably in the tournament, Jude and the Three Lions are knocked out in the World Cup quarter-finals against France.
May 2023	Dortmund just miss out on the *Bundesliga* title, losing out on goal difference to Bayern Munich on the last weekend of matches. Jude is named the *Bundesliga* Player of the Season.
14 June 2023	After three seasons at Dortmund, Jude signs for Real Madrid for one hundred and fifteen million pounds.
12 August 2023	He makes his debut for his new team against Athletic Bilbao, scoring with a half-volley.
August 2023	After scoring in each of his first four games, he is named *La Liga* Player of the Month.

28 October 2023	Jude scores twice in *El Clásico* against Barcelona, securing a famous 2-1 comeback win.
30 October 2023	Jude wins the *Kopa* Trophy for the world's best young player, at the *Ballon d'Or* ceremony in Paris.
14 January 2024	He helps his teammates smash Barcelona 4-1 in the Spanish Super Cup, securing his first club trophy with Real Madrid.

Bellingham's Clubs

BIRMINGHAM CITY FC

Nickname: the Blues

Founded: 1875

Current league: English Championship

Current manager: Tony Mowbray

Crest: two white spheres, one on top of the other, with a blue ribbon winding around them. The ribbon reads "Birmingham City Football Club 1875". The top sphere is a globe, the bottom sphere is a football.

BORUSSIA DORTMUND

Nickname: the Black and Yellows, the BVB

Founded: December 1909

Current league: German *Bundesliga*

Current manager: Edin Terzić

Crest: a yellow circle with black trim, with the letters BVB and the numbers zero and nine (BVB is short for *Ballspiel-Verein* Borussia Dortmund, the club's name; the numbers show the date the club was founded)

REAL MADRID CLUB DE FÚTBOL

Nickname: los Blancos (the Whites), los Merengues (the Meringues)

Founded: March 1902

Current league: *La Liga*

Current manager: Carlo Ancelotti

Crest: a yellow circle topped by a royal crown. Within the circle, the letters M, C and F (for Madrid Club de Fútbol) appear over a white and blue pattern.

TEAM HONOURS

England Under-17s: *Syrenka* Cup   2019

Borussia Dortmund: *DFB-Pokal Cup*   2021

England: European Championship   2021
runners-up medal

Real Madrid: Spanish Super Cup   2024

INDIVIDUAL HONOURS

Syrenka Cup Player of the Tournament:	2019
EFL Championship Young Player of the Month:	November 2019
Birmingham City Young Player of the Year:	2019/20
EFL Championship Young Player of the Year:	2019/20
Bundesliga Rookie of the Month:	September 2020
Bundesliga Goal of the Month:	October 2020/21

Bundesliga Players' Newcomer of the Season	2020/21
Bundesliga Team of the Season:	2021/22 and 2022/23
Bundesliga Player of the Season:	2022/23
Kopa Trophy: 2023	2023 (and runner-up in 2021)
Golden Boy:	2023
La Liga Player of the Month:	August 2023 and October 2023
Laureus World Sports Breakthrough of the Year	2024

JUDE IN PAINT

In February 2022, a huge mural appeared on the outside of the Ryemarket Shopping Centre in Stourbridge, the town where Jude was born. Painted by an artist called Gent 48, it showed Jude standing proudly in his England shirt, surrounded by smaller scenes of the player in his Birmingham and Dortmund days. There's also another mural of Jude near St Andrew's, including his famous line "Once a blue, always a blue"!

JUDE'S ENGLAND CAREER

Before moving up to the senior England team, Jude also played for four different national age groups:

England Under-15s (eight appearances, one goal) Debut: 17 December 2016 (aged thirteen years and five months)

England Under-16s (eleven appearances, three goals) Debut: 22 July 2018 (aged fifteen years and twenty-three days)

England Under-17s (three appearances, two goals) Debut: 6 September 2019 (aged sixteen years and two months)

England Under-21s (four appearances, one goal)
Debut: 4 September 2020 (aged seventeen years and two months)

TEN OF THE BEST BELLINGHAM GOALS:

14 September 2019: Birmingham City v Charlton Athletic: Striding calmly into the box, sixteen-year-old Jude meets a square pass and sends it low past the keeper, grabbing three away points for the Blues.

29 December 2019: Birmingham City v Leeds United: In a winter thriller at St Andrew's, which Leeds win 5-4, Jude stands out with a composed two-touch finish, trapping a cross then directing it neatly into the corner of the goal.

14 April 2021: Borussia Dortmund v Manchester City: In the big-match pressure of a Champions League quarter-final, Jude collects a ball just inside the area then fires a right-foot shot into the top corner, just beyond the reach of City keeper Ederson.

23 October 2021: Borussia Dortmund v Arminia Bielefeld: Jude shows his quality with a slaloming run into the box, weaving past three defenders then clipping the ball over the onrushing keeper. The goal is voted as *Bundesliga* Goal of the Month.

5 October 2022: Borussia Dortmund v Sevilla: Playing against Sevilla in the Champions League, Jude swerves right then left as he runs into the box, confusing the defenders, then slots the ball past the keeper from a tight angle.

21 November 2022: England v Iran: Jude gets his first international goal in England's opening World Cup match in Qatar, rising high to head a Luke Shaw cross into the net. It sets England up for a memorable 6-2 win.

22 January 2023: Borussia Dortmund v Augsburg: With defenders all around him on the edge of the box, Jude twists and turns to find space, then powers a shot just inside the post from twenty-five yards out. The keeper has no chance.

3 October 2023: Real Madrid v Napoli: Thirty-four minutes into an away Champions League game in Italy, Jude goes on a mazy run from near the halfway line, dodging through the Napoli defence then poking the ball past the keeper.

28 October 2023: Real Madrid v Barcelona: In the second half of his first ever appearance in *El Clásico*, Jude picks up the ball in midfield and sends a bullet of a shot high into the Barcelona goal, bringing Real Madrid level. An absolute screamer.

9 December 2023: Real Madrid v Real Betis In a tight, nervy match against Real Betis, Jude breaks the offside trap in the second half, running on to a through-ball, chesting it down, then slotting it firmly under the keeper. Classic Bellingham.

MARK BELLINGHAM: POLICEMAN, STRIKER AND FOOTBALL AGENT!

Agents do an important job for top footballers. They help to sort out contracts and salaries with big clubs, letting the players focus on training and playing. But while most footballers use professional agents, Jude takes a different approach – his agent is his dad!

That's right. Not only was Mark a police sergeant and a brilliant non-league striker, but he also acts as agent for his superstar son. He must be a good one, too – he managed to secure Jude a one-hundred-and-fifteen-million-pound transfer to Real Madrid!

JUDE QUOTES

On wearing Zidane's number five shirt at Real Madrid:
"I've always said how much I admire Zinedine Zidane. I'm not trying to be the same as him, as I'm just trying to be Jude, but it is a type of homage to a player I really appreciated when I was growing up. He was the best. I'm just trying to extend the legacy of the number."

On Jobe:
"My brother, Jobe, is a thoroughbred striker, just like our father. Watch out for him!"

On Birmingham City:
"Whatever happens, Birmingham City will always be my club and I will always be a blue."

On his mum, Denise:
"I think at the minute, the role my mum is playing for me is probably the biggest role of anyone, more than my coaches and managers, to be honest!"

On creating big moments on the pitch:
"I want to try and create memories that I'll remember forever, and that other people will remember forever. Memories live longer than any car or house you can buy. That's what motivates me."

On playing for the Three Lions:
"I'm proud to play for England every time I get the chance."

REAL RECORD BREAKER

On November 26, 2023, during a 3-0 victory against Cadiz, Jude scored his fourteenth goal of the season, setting a new record for the most goals scored by a Real Madrid player within their first fifteen games.

The previous record of thirteen goals was held by three legendary players: Cristiano Ronaldo, Alfredo di Stefano and Pruden.

A few months later, in April 2024, he scored the winner against Barcelona at the Bernabéu, becoming the only Real player to find the net in their first two *La Liga El Clásico* matches since Ruud van Nistelrooy in 2007."

FIVE FIVES

The number 5 shirt at Real Madrid is now worn by Jude, and was famously donned by Zinedine Zidane – one of the greatest players in history.

But the shirt hasn't always been so lucky for its wearer and the last five 5s before Jude had varying success.

Jesús Vallejo (21/22 to 22/23)

Raphaël Varane (16/17 to 20/21)

Fábio Coentrão (12/13 to 14/15)

Nuri Şahin (11/12)

Fernando Gago (09/10 to 10/11)

Also available in the Football Legends series:

FOOTBALL LEGENDS

HARRY KANE

Emily Hibbs

FOOTBALL LEGENDS

RAHEEM STERLING

Musa Okwonga

FOOTBALL LEGENDS

TAMMY ABRAHAM

Matt
Whyman

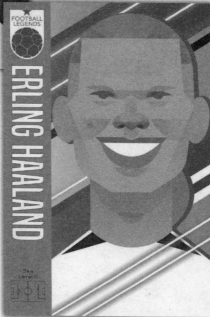

FOOTBALL LEGENDS

ERLING HAALAND

Ben
Lerwill

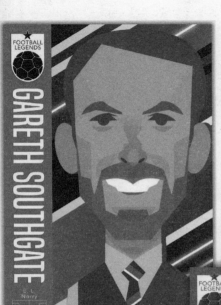

FOOTBALL LEGENDS

GARETH SOUTHGATE

E.L Norry

FOOTBALL LEGENDS

BUKAYO SAKA

Ben Lerwill